5038
This edition published in 2005 by John Hinde
© 1998 CLB International, Godalming, Surrey
ISBN 1-85833-809-3

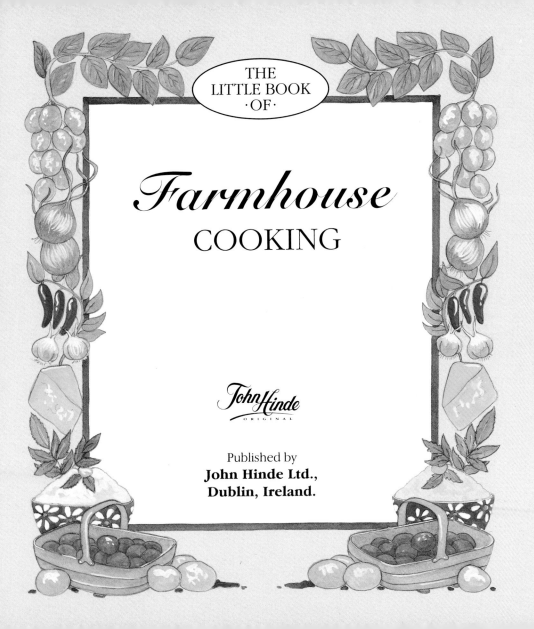

THE
LITTLE BOOK
·OF·

Farmhouse
COOKING

John Hinde
ORIGINAL

Published by
**John Hinde Ltd.,
Dublin, Ireland.**

Introduction

*F*armhouse cooking is all about using fresh, readily available produce to create dishes that are simple, wholesome and delicious. Traditional country food has never really disappeared from rural areas; it is simply that until recently the food industry has tended to ignore it in the rush to embrace the various exotic cuisines that are now so prevalent.

Thankfully this situation does seem to be changing, encouraged perhaps by many young chefs extolling the virtues of simple, fresh ingredients. At one time it was virtually impossible to eat in a restaurant and be served a really good quality meal unless it was French. Now, however, numerous cafés, restaurants and even pubs are serving an eclectic mix of recipes that are most definitely home-grown. Cookery schools such as Ballymaloe have only added to the drive towards a simpler, more fundamental form of cooking that has at its heart the idea that ingredients should be used when they are in season and at their very best.

The reason why farmhouse cooking has never been completely swamped by outside influences is quite understandable when we consider our history. Obviously this is how we would all have eaten at one time – by making the most of what we could grow, fish, raise or hunt. It makes economic sense to eat what is on our doorsteps and, of course, it is also

the simplest way to obtain the freshest possible ingredients. To many city-dwellers, however, the idea of farmhouse cooking conjures up images of slaving over an Aga for hours. This is only necessary if you actually want to cook in this manner: ask anyone who has had to cook three meals a day for six hungry men at lambing time, and you will find that the food may be wholesome and fresh but all manner of modern gadgetry will have been employed to prepare those meals.

This book offers a tempting selection of recipes that would grace the table of any farmhouse. Some, such as Carrot Soup or Chicken Cobbler, will be familiar as classic winter fare, while the more unusual recipes, such as Veal with Sorrel Stuffing or Roast Pork Wild Game Style illustrate the rich variety that is at the heart of country cooking.

Carrot Soup

SERVES 4

Carrots make a most delicious soup which is both filling and quick to prepare.

PREPARATION: 12 mins
COOKING: 25 mins

460g/1lb carrots
1 medium onion
1 medium turnip
2 cloves garlic, crushed
700ml/1¼ pints water or vegetable stock
½ tsp dried thyme
½ tsp ground nutmeg
Salt and ground white pepper, to taste
Toasted sunflower seeds, flaked almonds and
    pistachio nuts, mixed together for garnish

1. Peel the carrots and cut them into thick slices. Peel and roughly chop the onion and turnip.

2. Put the vegetables, garlic and water or stock, into a large saucepan and bring to the boil.

Step 1 Using a sharp knife, roughly chop the peeled onions and turnip.

Cover the pan, reduce the heat and simmer for 20 minutes.

3. Add the herbs and seasoning, and simmer for a further 5 minutes.

4. Using a liquidiser or food processor, blend the soup until it is thick and smooth.

5. Reheat the soup as required, garnishing with the seeds and nuts before serving.

Step 1 Cut the carrots into thick slices, approximately 1.25cm/½-inch thick.

Step 4 Purée the soup in a liquidiser or food processor, until it is thick and smooth.

Turkey Chowder

SERVES 6-8

Serve this good filling soup with crusty bread for a meal in itself.

PREPARATION: 15 mins
COOKING: 3½ hrs

Turkey bones
1 bay leaf
3 black peppercorns
1 blade of mace
1 onion, unpeeled
200g/7oz pearl barley, rinsed
3 stalks celery, sliced
3 carrots, diced
175g/6oz green beans, sliced
150g/5oz canned sweetcorn, drained
2 tbsps chopped parsley

---

1. Use the carcass from a roast turkey. Break up the carcass and place in a large pot with any skin and leftover meat, the bay leaf, peppercorns, mace and onion.

2. Pour in 2.3 litres/4 pints cold water to cover the bones, and then cover the pot. Bring to the boil, then simmer, partially covered, for about 2 hours.

3. Strain and reserve the stock. Remove any meat from the bones, dice and reserve.

4. Combine the strained stock, barley, celery, carrots and green beans. Partially cover and bring to the boil, then reduce the heat and simmer for 1-1½ hrs, or until the barley is tender. Add the corn after about 45 minutes cooking time, and stir in the chopped parsley and any diced turkey.

Watercress and Mushroom Pâté

SERVES 4

A delightful pâté served with thinly sliced brown bread.

PREPARATION: 10 mins
COOKING: 5 mins

30g/1oz butter
1 medium onion, finely chopped
90g/3oz dark, flat mushrooms, finely chopped
1 bunch watercress, finely chopped
120g/4oz low fat curd cheese
Few drops soy sauce
Scant ½ tsp caraway seeds
Black pepper

1. Melt the butter over a low heat and cook the onion until soft but not coloured.

Step 3 Put in the chopped watercress and stir for about 30 seconds until it becomes limp.

Step 7 Put into individual ramekin dishes or one large serving dish and chill for 2 hours.

2. Raise the heat, add the mushrooms and cook quickly for 2 minutes.

3. Put in the chopped watercress and stir for about 30 seconds until it becomes limp.

4. Place the contents of the pan in a blender together with the cheese and soy sauce.

5. Blend until smooth, stirring the mixture if necessary.

6. Stir in the caraway seeds and pepper to taste.

7. Put into individual ramekin dishes or one large serving dish and chill for at least 2 hours until firm.

Salmon Trout with Spinach

SERVES 6-8

This dish is perfect for a special occasion.

PREPARATION: 35-40 mins
COOKING: 40 mins

1.1kg/2½lb fresh whole salmon trout, cleaned
900g/2lbs spinach, stalks removed
1 small onion, finely chopped
60g/2oz polyunsaturated margarine
60g/2oz walnuts, roughly chopped
120g/4oz fresh white breadcrumbs
1 tbsp fresh chopped parsley
1 tbsp fresh chopped thyme
¼ tsp grated nutmeg
Salt and freshly ground black pepper
Juice of 2 lemons
Watercress sprigs and lemon slices, to garnish

---

1. Carefully cut the underside of the fish to the tip of the tail. Sit it, belly side down, spreading the cut underside out to balance it.

2. Using the palm of your hand press down along the backbone, pushing the spine downwards. Turn the fish over and using a sharp knife, carefully pull the backbone away, cutting it out with scissors at the base of the head and tail.

3. Pull out any loose bones with a pair of tweezers then set the fish in the centre of a large square of lightly oiled foil.

4. Put the washed spinach into a large saucepan and sprinkle with salt. Do not add any extra water. Cover and cook over a moderate heat for about 3 minutes.

5. Turn into a colander and drain well, pressing with a spoon to remove all the excess moisture. Chop very finely using a sharp knife.

6. Fry the onion gently in 15g/2½oz of the margarine until soft. Stir into the spinach along with the walnuts, breadcrumbs, herbs, nutmeg, salt, pepper and half the lemon juice. Mix well.

7. Push the stuffing firmly into the cavity of the fish, re-shaping it as you do so. Seal the foil over the fish, but do not wrap too tightly. Place in a roasting tin and bake in a preheated oven at 180°C/350°F/Gas Mark 4, for 35 minutes.

8. Carefully unwrap the fish and transfer to a large serving dish. Using a sharp knife, peel away the exposed skin of the fish.

9. Dot with the remaining margarine, sprinkle with the remaining lemon juice, and garnish.

Chicken Cobbler

SERVES 6

A warming winter dish with a creamy sauce and light topping.

PREPARATION: 25 mins
COOKING: 1 hr

---

4 chicken joints, 2 breasts and 2 legs
1.5 litres/2½ pints water
1 bay leaf
4 whole peppercorns
2 carrots, peeled and diced
24 button onions, peeled
90g/6 tbsps frozen sweetcorn
140ml/¼ pint double cream

Topping
400g/14oz plain flour
1½ tbsps baking powder
Pinch salt
5 tbsps butter or margarine
340ml/12 fl oz milk
1 egg, beaten with a pinch of salt

---

1. Place the chicken in a deep saucepan with water, bay leaf and peppercorns. Cover and bring to the boil. Reduce the heat and allow to simmer for 20-30 minutes, or until the chicken is tender. Remove the chicken from the pot and allow to cool. Skim and discard the fat from the surface of the stock. Skin the chicken and remove the meat from the bones.

Step 5 Roll out the mixture on a floured surface, cut into rounds and place on top of the chicken mixture.

2. Continue to simmer the stock until reduced by about half. Strain, then add the carrots and onions. Cook until tender and add the sweetcorn. Stir in the cream and season. Add the chicken. Pour into a casserole.

3. To prepare the topping, sift the dry ingredients into a bowl.

4. Rub in the butter or margarine until the mixture resembles small peas. Stir in enough of the milk to bind the mixture.

5. Turn out onto a floured surface and knead lightly. Roll out with a floured rolling pin and cut with a pastry cutter. Brush the surface of each round with the egg mixture. Place on top of the chicken mixture and bake for 10-15 minutes in a pre-heated oven at 190°C/375°F/ Gas Mark 5. Serve immediately.

Veal with Sorrel Stuffing

SERVES 6

Fresh sorrel has a delightful flavour, if it is not available use fresh spinach instead.

PREPARATION: 25 mins
COOKING: 1 hr

900g/2lbs rolled joint of veal
120g/4oz low fat soft cheese with garlic and
  herbs
120g/4oz sorrel, finely chopped
2 tsps fresh oregano or marjoram, chopped
60g/2oz walnuts, finely chopped
Freshly ground black pepper
60g/2oz plain flour
½ tsp paprika
1 egg, beaten
120g/4oz dried breadcrumbs
45g/1½oz polyunsaturated margarine, melted

---

1. Unroll the veal joint and trim off some of the fat from the outside using a sharp knife.

2. Put the cheese, sorrel, oregano or marjoram, walnuts and black pepper into a bowl. Mix

Step 2 Spread the filling ingredients evenly over the inside of the joint of meat.

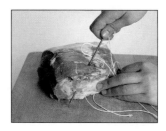

Step 2 Sew the ends of the joint together using a trussing needle and strong thread.

together using a round bladed knife or your hands, until the ingredients are well bound together. Spread this filling over the inside of the veal. Roll the veal joint up, swiss-roll fashion, and sew the ends together with a trussing needle and thick thread.

3. Dredge the veal roll with the flour and sprinkle with the paprika. Press this coating well onto the meat using your hands.

4. Brush the floured joint liberally with beaten egg and roll it into the dried breadcrumbs, pressing gently to make sure that all surfaces are thoroughly coated.

5. Place the coated veal on a baking sheet, brush with the melted margarine and roast in a preheated oven at 160°C/325°F/Gas Mark 5, for 1 hour, or until the meat is well cooked.

6. Allow to stand for 10 minutes before slicing and serving hot, or chill and serve cold.

Kidneys with Mustard Sauce

SERVES 4

Lambs' kidneys have a delicate flavour, which a mustard sauce complements perfectly.

PREPARATION: 25 mins
COOKING: 15 mins

4 tbsps vegetable oil
675g/1½lbs lambs' kidneys
1-2 shallots, peeled and finely chopped
280ml/½ pint dry white wine
3 tbsps Dijon mustard
Salt, pepper and lemon juice, to taste
2 tbsps fresh chopped parsley

1. Cut the kidneys in half lengthways, and carefully snip out the core and tough tubes.

2. Heat the oil in a large frying pan, and gently sauté the kidneys for about 10 minutes, stirring them frequently until they are light brown on all sides. Remove the kidneys from the pan and keep them warm.

Step 1 Trim any fat or tubes away from the core of each kidney, using a sharp knife or small pair of scissors.

Step 2 Sauté the kidneys in the hot oil, stirring them frequently to brown evenly on all sides.

3. Add the shallots to the sauté pan and cook for about 1 minute, stirring frequently until they soften.

4. Add the wine and bring to the boil, stirring constantly and scraping the pan to remove any brown juices.

5. Allow the wine to boil rapidly for 3-4 minutes, until it has reduced by about half. Remove the pan from the heat.

6. Using a balloon whisk or fork, mix the mustard into the reduced wine along with salt, pepper, lemon juice to taste, and half of the fresh chopped parsley.

7. Return the kidneys to the pan and cook over a low heat for 1-2 minutes, stirring all the time to heat the kidneys through evenly. Serve immediately, sprinkled with the remaining parsley.

Roast Pork in Wild Game Style

SERVES 6-8

The love of game is part of Polish culinary history and even meat from domestic animals was often given the same treatment.

PREPARATION: 20 mins, plus 2 days marinating
COOKING: 2¼ hrs

1.4kg/3lb boneless joint of pork
60g/2oz lard or dripping
Paprika
1 tsp flour
175ml/6 fl oz soured cream or thick yogurt
1 tbsp chopped fresh dill

Marinade
1 carrot, finely chopped
2 celery sticks, finely chopped
1 bay leaf
5 black peppercorns
5 allspice berries
2 sprigs thyme
10 juniper berries, slightly crushed
2 onions, sliced
140ml/¼ pint dry white wine
Juice and grated rind of 1 lemon

Beetroot accompaniment
900g/2lbs cooked beetroot, peeled
60g/2oz butter or margarine
2 tbsps flour
1 onion, finely chopped
1 clove garlic, crushed
140ml/¼ pint chicken stock
Sugar, salt and pepper
White wine vinegar

---

1. Combine the marinade ingredients in a saucepan and bring to the boil. Allow to cool. Place the pork in a bowl and pour over the marinade. Cover and refrigerate for two days, turning the meat frequently. Remove the meat and wipe it dry with kitchen paper. Reserve the marinade.

2. Heat the lard in a roasting tin. Sprinkle the fat side of the pork with paprika, and brown it on all sides. Cook, uncovered, in an oven preheated to 190°C/375°F/Gas Mark 5, for 2 hours. Pour over the marinade after one hour. Baste frequently with the pan juices.

3. Remove the pork from the tin and keep warm. Skim any fat from the sauce and strain the vegetables and juice into a pan. Mix the flour, soured cream, and dill together and add to the pan. Bring just to the boil, then simmer for 1-2 minutes.

4. Grate the beetroot or cut it into small dice. Melt the butter in a saucepan and add the flour and onion. Stir well and cook over a moderate heat until light brown. Add the garlic and stir in the stock gradually.

5. Bring to the boil, add the beetroot, sugar, salt, pepper, and vinegar to taste. Cook for 10 minutes over a moderate heat, stirring occasionally.

6. To serve, slice the pork and pour over the sauce. Serve with the beetroot.

Winter Crumble

SERVES 4-6

A variety of hearty vegetables topped with oats and cheese makes the perfect winter meal.

PREPARATION: 20 mins
COOKING: 1 hr 5 mins

Topping
90g/3oz butter or margarine
120g/4oz wholewheat flour
60g/2oz rolled oats
120/4oz Cheddar cheese, grated
1/4 tsp salt

Filling
175ml/6 fl oz stock or water
280ml/½ pint sweet cider
1 tsp brown sugar
2 carrots, chopped
2 large parsnips, cut into rings
2 sticks celery, chopped
2 heads broccoli, cut into florets
¼ cauliflower, cut into florets
1 tbsps wholewheat flour
2 tbsps chopped parsley
1 medium onion, chopped and fried until
   golden
4 large tomatoes, skinned and chopped
225g/8oz cooked black-eyed beans

---

1. Make the topping by rubbing the butter into the flour and oats until the mixture resembles fine breadcrumbs. Stir in the cheese and salt.

Step 1 Rub the butter into the flour and oats until the mixture resembles fine breadcrumbs.

2. Mix the stock with the cider and sugar and put into a large pan with the carrots and parsnips.

3. Cook until just tender, remove the vegetables and put aside.

4. Add the celery, broccoli and cauliflower to the pan, cook until tender, remove and reserve.

5. Mix the flour with a little water, add to the cider and cook until thickened, stirring all the time. Add the parsley.

6. Place the onions, vegetables, tomatoes and beans in a greased casserole and season well. Pour the sauce over the mixture.

7. Sprinkle the topping over the top and press down a little.

8. Cook at 200°C/400°F/Gas Mark 6 for 30-35 minutes or until the topping is golden brown.

Herbed Vegetable Strips

SERVES 4

Fresh basil and parsley mixed with tender-crisp vegetables and nuts make a delicious side dish.

PREPARATION: 30-40 mins
COOKING: 10 mins

2 large courgettes, ends trimmed
2 medium carrots, peeled
1 large or 2 small leeks, trimmed, halved and
   well washed
120g/4oz walnuts
1 small onion, chopped
2 tbsps chopped parsley
2 tbsps chopped basil
280-420ml/½-¾ pint olive oil
Salt and pepper

1. Cut the courgettes and carrots into long, thin slices with a mandolin or by hand. A food processor will work but the slices will be short.

2. Cut the leeks into lengths the same size as the courgettes and carrots. Make sure the leeks are well rinsed in between all layers. Cut into long, thin strips.

3. Using a large, sharp knife, cut the courgette and carrot slices into long, thin strips about the thickness of 2 matchsticks. The julienne blade of a food processor will produce strips that are too fine to use.

4. Place the carrot strips in a pan of boiling salted water and cook for about 3-4 minutes or until tender-crisp. Drain and rinse under cold

Step 3 Stack up several lengths of courgette and carrot and cut into long julienne strips.

water. Cook the courgette strips separately for about 2-3 minutes and add the leek strips during the last minute of cooking. Drain and rinse the vegetables and leave with the carrots to drain dry.

5. Place the walnuts, onion, parsley and basil in the bowl of a food processor or in a blender and chop finely.

6. Reserve about 3 tbsps of the olive oil for later use. With the machine running, pour the rest of the oil through the funnel in a thin, steady stream. Use enough oil to bring the mixture to the consistency of mayonnaise. Add seasoning to taste.

7. Heat the reserved oil in a large pan and add the vegetables. Season and toss over moderate heat until heated through. Add the herb and walnut sauce and toss gently to coat the vegetables. Serve immediately.

Brown Bread Crumble

SERVES 2

The unusual crumble topping on this dessert is simple to make, high in fibre and very tasty.
Serve with custard or cream for a treat.

PREPARATION: 15 mins
COOKING: 20 mins

175g/6oz cooking apples, cored and sliced
120g/4oz raspberries
60g/2oz fresh wholemeal breadcrumbs
60g/2oz rolled oats
45g/1½oz light muscovado sugar
½ tsp ground cinnamon
¼ tsp ground cardamom
45g/1½oz butter or margarine

---

1. Arrange the apple slices in a small pie dish and scatter the raspberries over the top.

2. Put the breadcrumbs, oats, sugar and spices in a large bowl. Mix together well to distribute the spices evenly.

3. Add the butter and rub into the mixture until well mixed.

4. Spoon the topping over the prepared fruit and smooth the top with a spoon.

5. Bake in an oven preheated to 190°C/375°F/ Gas Mark 5, for 20-25 minutes or until the topping is lightly browned and the filling piping hot.

Apple Nut Tart

SERVES 6

The sweet, spicy flavour of cinnamon blends perfectly with the apples and nuts in this traditional dessert.

PREPARATION: 20 mins
COOKING: 40 mins

250g/9oz plain flour
150g/5oz caster sugar
135g/4½oz butter, cut into pieces
1 egg
460g/1lb dessert apples, peeled, cored and
 sliced
60g/2oz hazelnuts, coarsely ground
1 tsp ground cinnamon
Juice of 1 lemon
3 tbsps apricot brandy (optional)
120g/4oz apricot jam, melted
60g/2oz chopped hazelnuts

---

1. Sieve together the flour and 120g/4oz of the sugar into a bowl. Rub in the butter until the mixture resembles fine breadcrumbs.

Step 4 Layer the apples and ground hazelnuts in the pastry case.

Step 5 Pour the melted jam over the layers of apples and hazelnuts.

2. Make a well in the centre of the flour mixture and drop in the egg. Gradually incorporate the flour into the egg using a knife or, as the mixture becomes firmer, your fingers. Continue kneading the mixture together, until it forms a smooth dough.

3. Wrap the dough in cling film and chill for at least 30 minutes, then roll out and use it to line a 20cm/8-inch greased flan tin.

4. Layer the apple slices and the ground hazelnuts in the pastry case. Sprinkle over the cinnamon, remaining sugar, lemon juice and apricot brandy, if using.

5. Pour the melted jam over, and sprinkle with the chopped hazelnuts. Bake in a preheated oven at 220°C/425°F/Gas Mark 7, for 35-40 minutes or until the fruit is soft and the tart is golden brown.

Carrot Cake with Apricot Filling

SERVES 6-8

This tasty cake will freeze well for up to 2 months.

PREPARATION: 20 mins
COOKING: 45-50 mins

120g/4oz dried apricots
175g/6oz butter or margarine
175g/6oz brown sugar
2 eggs, separated
200g/7oz plain flour
1 tsp baking powder
225g/8oz carrots (150g/5oz weight when peeled and finely grated)
60g/2oz sultanas
90g/3oz walnuts, finely chopped
2 tsps grated lemon rind
½ tsp ground cinnamon

1. Soak the apricots in water overnight, drain and purée until smooth.

2. Beat the butter and sugar together until pale and creamy.

3. Whisk the egg yolks and beat into the butter and sugar.

4. Sieve the flour and baking powder and fold into the mixture.

5. Fold in the rest of the ingredients except the egg whites.

6. Whisk the egg whites until they form soft peaks, and fold into the mixture.

7. Place the mixture in a greased 18cm/7-inch round spring-form cake tin. Bake in an oven preheated to 180°C/350°F/Gas Mark 4, for 45-50 minutes.

8. Cool in the tin for 10 minutes and then turn out onto a wire rack.

9. When completely cooled, slice in half and sandwich together with the apricot purée.

Chocolate Apple Cake

MAKES 1 × 18CM/8-INCH CAKE

This cake is nicer if kept in an airtight tin for a day before serving.

PREPARATION: 25 mins
COOKING: 1¼ hrs

150g/5oz butter, softened or soft margarine
120g/4oz light muscavado sugar
1 large egg, beaten
175g/6oz fine wholemeal flour
90g/3oz cocoa powder
1½ tsps baking powder
1 tbsp Amontillado sherry
400g/14oz Bramley cooking apples, peeled and
   sliced

Topping
120g/4oz chocolate chips
Knob of butter
A little water

1. Cream the butter and sugar together until fluffy.

2. Add half of the beaten egg and continue creaming.

3. Fold in the rest of the egg together with the sieved flour, cocoa and baking powder and sherry.

4. Place half of the mixture into a round 18cm/8-inch cake tin and cover with the sliced apples.

5. Add the other half of the mixture and smooth the top.

6. Bake in an oven preheated to 160°C/325°F/Gas Mark 3, for 1¼ hours or until firm to the touch.

7. Melt the chocolate chips with the butter and water and drizzle over the top of the cake.

Wholewheat Bread

MAKES 2 LOAVES

This very moist bread, which uses no yeast, will last for days. If wished add some caraway seeds to the dough before baking and sprinkle some on top of the loaves to decorate.

PREPARATION: 20 mins
COOKING: 1¼-1½hrs

680g/1½ lbs wholewheat flour
120g/4oz white flour
100g/3½oz porridge oats
60g/2oz bran
175g/6oz pinhead oatmeal
60g/2oz wheatgerm
½ tsp baking powder
½ tsp sea salt
2 eggs, beaten
1.2 litres/2 pints milk

1. Mix all the dry ingredients together in a large bowl and make a well in the centre.

2. Add the eggs and milk to the well in the dry ingredients and gradually incorporate the dry ingredients into the liquid until all is well blended.

3. Spoon into 2 greased 500g/1lb loaf tins and bake in the centre of an oven preheated to 180°C/350°F/Gas Mark 4, for 1¼-1½ hours. When cooked, the loaves should sound hollow when tapped underneath.

4. Turn out of the tins to cool on a wire rack.

Granary Rolls

For a crisp crust brush the rolls with salted water and sprinkle with cracked wheat before baking.

PREPARATION: 1 hr
COOKING: 15-20 mins

340g/12oz granary flour
1 tsp salt
15g/½oz fresh yeast or 2 tsps dried yeast
1 tsp brown sugar
225ml/8 fl oz warm water
30g/1oz vegetable fat, melted

---

1. Place the flour and salt in a mixing bowl and leave in a warm place.

2. Cream the yeast and sugar together with three-quarters of the warm water.

3. Make a well in the middle of the flour and pour in the yeast mixture.

4. Add the melted fat and mix to a pliable dough, adding the remaining water as necessary.

5. Knead lightly for a minute or two, then cover with a clean damp tea-towel and leave in a warm place until the dough has doubled in size.

6. Knead again for 3-5 minutes and shape into 10 smooth rolls.

7. Place well apart on a floured baking tray, cover and leave in a warm place until the rolls have doubled in size.

8. Bake in the centre of an oven preheated to 220°C/425°F/Gas Mark 7, for 15-20 minutes or until the rolls sound hollow when tapped underneath. Cool on a wire rack.

Rhubarb and Raspberry Jam

MAKES About 9 cups

Raspberries can be expensive, but when mixed with rhubarb, just a few will produce a delicious fruity jam. Black or red raspberries or loganberries can be used.

PREPARATION: 30 mins
COOKING: 40 mins

3 cups rhubarb, cut into small pieces
⅔ cup water
6 cups raspberries
3 tbsps lemon juice
6 cups sugar

1. Place the rhubarb with the water, in a preserving pan and simmer gently 10 minutes or until the rhubarb is just soft.

2. Add the raspberries and lemon juice, and continue to cook 10 minutes or until all the fruit is very soft.

3. Stir in the sugar, and cook gently stirring

Cut the rhubarb into even-sized pieces about ½ inch long.

until all the sugar has dissolved.

4. Boil rapidly until setting point is reached; some spooned onto a cold plate and left for 2 minutes should wrinkle when tilted.

5. Allow to stand 20 minutes then stir. Pour into hot, sterilized jars, seal and label.

Piccalilli

MAKES About 1kg/2¼lbs

A traditional English pickle. Any vegetables can be used, but this combination works well.

PREPARATION: 20 mins, plus 6 hrs standing
COOKING: 15-20 mins

340g/12oz pickling cucumbers, diced
340g/12oz onions, chopped
340g/12oz cauliflower, cut into small florets
1 large green pepper, diced
Salt
280ml/½ pint distilled malt vinegar
2 tbsps yellow mustard
½ tsp turmeric
½ tsp mustard seeds
¼ tsp dried thyme
1 bay leaf
60g/2oz sugar
1 tbsp cornflour mixed with a little water

1. Layer the vegetables in a dish, sprinkle each layer liberally with salt.

2. Leave for at least 6 hours to draw out water from the vegetables. Rinse and drain well.

3. Place the vegetables in a large saucepan or preserving pan and add the vinegar, mustard, turmeric, mustard seeds, thyme, bay leaf and sugar.

4. Stir to mix well. Bring gently to the boil and simmer for 8 minutes, or until the vegetables are cooked but still crisp.

5. Stir in the cornflour mixture and cook until thickened.

6. Pour into hot, sterilized jars, then seal with acid-proof lids and label. Store refrigerated.

Index

Wholewheat Bread